THE ULTIMATE

BEGINNERS GUIDE TO

CRYPTOCURRENCIES

An introduction to crypto-currencies

and the technologies that powers them

By

Fito Kahn

For permissions contact:

info@cryptocurrencyinfo.today

Cryptocurrency Info Today
6200 Yaupon Dr.
Austin, TX 78759
www.cryptocurrencyinfo.today

Ordering Information:
Quantity sales. Special discounts are available on quantity purchases by corporations, associations and others. For details, email publisher or contact the publisher at the address above.

Cover Photo by Fito Kahn

Cover Design by Faiza (Fizart_gallary)

Disclaimer

This book and the content provided herein are simply for educational purposes and do not take the place of legal advice from your attorney. Every effort has been made to ensure that the content provided in this book is accurate and helpful for our readers at publishing time. However, this is not an exhaustive treatment of the subjects. No liability is assumed for losses or damages due to the information provided. You are responsible for your own choices, actions and results. You should consult your attorney for your specific publishing and disclaimer questions and needs.

ISBN: 978-1-54398-284-8

Dedication

To my wife, Judy, my daughters Leslie, Lauren
and Lindsey and my grandchildren Aubrey,
McKinley, Ava, Caden and Brooklyn.
I dedicate this book to you.
You all are my reason, purpose and inspiration.

Now go buy some Bitcoin!

TABLE OF CONTENTS

INTRODUCTION

The 80s is where my story begins. The age of personal computers. In the early 80's, I owned a chain of computer stores. My stores sold some of the first personal computers like the Apple II computers, the Atari, the first IBM PCs, the Commodore Pet, Vic 20 and the 64, the first Hewlett Packard computers and the first Compaq personal computer, as well as, many others. In the early 80s, it seemed like every company was coming out with a personal computer. Some companies would make it and become successful but many companies would not and now their computers are only remembered and seen in computer museums. This scenario will soon repeat itself in the following decades, as we will see.

Some of you all remember those early days of personal computing. The personal computer was a new frontier. It was the wild west. We all were learning about bits and bytes, disk drives, RAM and ROM memory, monitors and floppy disks. The first spreadsheet, Visicalc and the first popular word processor, Wordstar and Dbase II one of the first databases entered our world and our vocabularies. On December 26, 1982, Time Magazine awarded its "Man of the Year" award to the personal computer calling it "Machine of the Year". This was the first time the magazine had given the award to a non-human since the magazine began in 1927.

Soon we heard about something called the Internet.

The Internet back then was another new technology that few people knew about, understood or used. Slowly, we began to hear things about this network of connected computers. We soon heard about something called the World Wide Web and things called URLs, words like webpages, email and chat rooms soon began to creep into our vocabulary.

In the early '90s, with the growing popularity of the Internet, I saw that the Internet was going to be big once it was easier to use and people could understand its potential. I jumped right in and began learning how to build websites when I saw a demonstration of NCSA's Mosaic browser. I was hooked as soon as I saw it.

How many of you remember using a 300 baud modem to connect to the Internet?

Remember how we had it connected to our phone and if someone picked up we would lose connection? What could you do back then on the Internet? Not much... until we had our first browsers. Remember AOL?

Fast forward to 2009

In 2009, I first heard about a cryptocurrency called Bitcoin that you created by "mining" . You ran some software on your computer that would create these tokens or coins. Anytime your software solved a mathematical problem you got some Bitcoins. At the time, I did not think much about Bitcoin or its potential. The only people involved with Bitcoin at the time were computer geeks and hackers and there was not much you could do with Bitcoin once you had them. Imagine being able to make and collect your own marbles. That is what I imagined. Having a bunch of marbles that I could not really do anything with. If I had only known then what I know now!

An important event took place in May 2010 – A computer programmer and Bitcoin miner named Laszlo Hanyecz, who lived in the US, had accumulated a large number of Bitcoins but did not know what to do with them. He sent out an email to his hacker buddies offering 10,000 Bitcoins for two pizzas. He was able to find someone in England who took him up on his offer. This person called a Papa John's Pizza in Jacksonville, Florida and ordered two pizzas for delivery to Laszlo. Those pizzas cost the guy in England less than $50 and that was the first time Bitcoin was used to buy something of value. At that time, it was calculated that a Bitcoin was worth 0.0025 cents! I don't know what happened to the guy with the 10,000 Bitcoins but today with Bitcoin trading at over $10,000 a Bitcoin, what would those 10,000 Bitcoins be worth? I would say that $100 million for those 2 pizzas was a great swap.

So anyway, I forgot about Bitcoin and went on with my life selling computers, building websites and raising a family until one day in late 2016, a friend told me about Bitcoin again. Bitcoin was now at $800 per Bitcoin. What! That can't be the same Bitcoin that I saw back in 2009? I started doing more research and realized that there was now more than just hackers getting into and using Bitcoin.

There was now an infrastructure developing around Bitcoin. There was a large, excited and dedicated community out there that was deeply involved in promoting and using Bitcoin. There were meetups and conferences and conventions happening all over the world. Some businesses had started accepting Bitcoin as payment for goods and services. There were now ATMs that dispensed Bitcoin, as well! There were money exchanges where you could easily buy and sell Bitcoin and convert your Bitcoin to cash and most surprising to me, you could even buy Bitcoin and put it in an IRA!

By the time I decided to purchase some Bitcoin in early 2017, the price of a Bitcoin was now at $1000 each! This is when I realized that I had found an incredible new industry that was still in its infancy. This industry was growing slowly and under the radar but had the potential to grow into something as big and as disruptive as the Internet had been just 30 years earlier. I found myself getting more excited and more passionate about Bitcoin. I read everything I could about Bitcoin, cryptocurrencies, Blockchain, Smart Contracts and anything else I could get my hands on that talked about this new space. I become an advocate for everything Bitcoin and cryptocurrency-related. I started buying Bitcoin and other cryptocurrencies, attending Bitcoin conferences, local meetups and even started an educational cryptocurrency website to help people learn about and get started in cryptocurrencies. This book is a record of my journey into cryptocurrencies and what I have learned along the way.

I am excited that you are wanting to learn more about these exciting new technologies. My hope is that after reading the book, you'll get the crypto bug like I have. I've made it my mission to teach as many people as possible about why we should all be learning and getting involved with cryptocurrencies. I think that this is the perfect time to get involved.

My objective with this book is to share my knowledge of what I have learned in this new space and also what I think is coming and how we can all be better prepared and informed about these new technologies. This book contains some great basic information, valuable tips, great resources and some insights as to what we can expect to see happening in the next few years.

I'm including chapters on some new technology terms and their definitions, a brief history of cryptocurrencies, how they work at a semi-technical level and how they are set to transform and affect our money, business, government and society, as well as, why we should be paying attention to them now. The chapter on terms is especially important that you become familiar with now that you are embarking on this journey to learn all about cryptocurrencies.

Finally, I've included a chapter on some interesting and popular cryptocurrencies that you might want to look into and keep an eye on.

Navigating this new world of cryptocurrencies, Blockchains and smart contracts can be a very daunting task due to the vast amount of information and misinformation out there when you surf the Internet. Add to that the use of new terminology, crypto technical concepts and the relative infancy of the crypto space in general and it can be very hard to find resources to help you learn and understand. I hope this book will be a good starting point to help you attain this knowledge.

Chapter 1. The Internet

The Internet has changed the face of communications, information, music, entertainment and gaming industries. Companies like Apple, Facebook, Netflix, HomeAway, Amazon and Google made and continue to make millions of dollars yearly using the Internet. It has totally changed the world.

With the advent of the Internet, we had to learn about many new technologies and innovations. We also had to learn a whole new vocabulary. Words like email, browsers, CPUs, hard drives, bytes, megabytes, gigabytes, URLs, modems and many other words entered into our vocabulary. We soon began to use these words daily. The Internet and its associated terminologies and vocabulary are now mainstream and ubiquitous. Computers, tablets and smartphones are found everywhere. Children now walk around with their iPads using them for everything from learning, educational games, listening to their favorite music, watching videos and even using them as a sound machine to help them to go to sleep.

By 2017, over 51% of the world's population had access to the Internet. As of April 2019, that number has jumped to over 56%[1]. Around 52.4% of the global online population access the

---

[1] By Jeff Ogden (W163) - Own work, based on figures from the Wikipedia:List of countries by number of Internet users article in the English Wikipedia, which is in turn based on figures from the International Telecommunications Union (ITU) for 2010 (updated to

Internet from their mobile devices and more than half of the global population is estimated to go online using mobile devices by 2020. These statistics mean that the world is already prepared for the next technological wave. The way that people communicate more and more is on their smart devices. The way many people in the world access the Internet is through their smart device and the way many people all over the world are transacting with their banks is through their smart device, as well. Soon people all over the world will be handling their financial transactions directly without the need of a bank. Many people now think that this will be inevitable outcome.

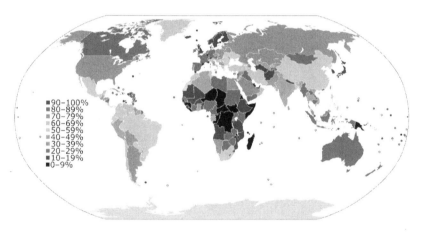

Internet users in 2015 as a%age of a country's population

Fast forward to 2019. We are at the beginning of one of the largest technological revolutions since the Internet. Many think of this new revolution as Internet 2.0 and believe that it will have just as much of an impact as the Internet of the 90s did, if not even greater.

The emerging technologies of the Blockchain, cryptocurrencies and smart contracts are set to disrupt the finance, real estate, shipping, insurance, transportation, food and healthcare sectors and will even replace how we vote, exchange assets, pay our taxes, receive our Social Security and Medicare payments, as well as how we purchase many of our goods and services. We have some exciting times ahead of us and it is important that we understand not only what these emerging technologies are but how we can prepare to use them.

Before we get started, I would like to lay a little groundwork and make sure that we understand something about what got us here. For that, we have to start at the beginning and that beginning is money…

Chapter 2. Money

While doing my research for this book, I came across some interesting facts about money and thought that it might be a good idea to include some of them in the book. You can never have enough fun facts that you can share at the next party you attend.

INTERESTING FACTS ABOUT MONEY

- The word salary comes from the Latin solarium Argentum(salt)[2].
- Roman soldiers were partially paid in salt[3].
- A Roman soldiers salary was cut if he was "not worth his salt".[4]
- In early North America, a beaver pelt could buy 2 pounds of sugar, a brass kettle, a gallon or brandy, a pair of shoes or 8 knives.[5]
- Deer or "buckskins" were commonly sold and traded. This led to the slang term for a currency called "a buck".[6]
- In Italy, as early as the year 1200 a.d, wheels of parmesan cheese were used as a medium of exchange[7]

---

[2] https://www.saltassociation.co.uk/education/salt-history/roman-times/
[3] https://www.saltassociation.co.uk/education/salt-history/roman-times/
[4] http://kiwihellenist.blogspot.com/2017/01/salt-and-salary.html
[5] http://digital.library.mcgill.ca/nwc/history/01.htm
[6] https://www.investopedia.com/terms/b/buck.asp
[7] http://money.visualcapitalist.com/the-worlds-strangest-currencies/

- The cost to produce, administer and distribute the 5-cent coin in 2017 was 6.60 cents[8].
- 94% of paper money is contaminated with harmful bacteria.[9]
- U.S. paper money is not made of paper. It's a material made of a cotton blend.[10]
- The Romans made their coins in the temple of Juno Moneta, the goddess of marriage and women. From the name, Moneta derives the words "mint" and "money".[11]

SOBERING FACTS ABOUT MONEY

- If you have $10 in your pocket and no debt, you are wealthier than 25% of Americans.[12]
- 96% of employed people will not be able to retire at age 65[13]
- 29% of households have less than $1,000 in savings.[14]
- Governments can only get money in three ways: 1) by printing, 2) by borrowing or 3) by collecting taxes from their citizens.[15]

---

[8] http://www.coinnews.net/2018/02/26/penny-costs-1-82-cents-to-make-in-2017/
[9] http://moneyversed.com/absurd-money-facts/
[10] https://www.aol.com/2010/11/23/10-fascinating-facts-about-u-s-currency/
[11] https://www.revolvy.com/page/Moneta
[12] http://moneyversed.com/absurd-money-facts/
[13] http://moneyversed.com/absurd-money-facts/

[14] https://www.cnbc.com/2018/09/27/heres-how-much-money-americans-have-in-savings-at-every-income-level.html
[15] https://benjaminstudebaker.com/2015/05/12/the-3-ways-governments-raise-money-part-i-taxation/

- The worst market crash in the United States lasted two years (1930-1932) and helped spawn the Great Depression. A thousand dollars invested in September 1929 was worth just $108.14 in July 1932[16]
- Due to hyperinflation, the government of Hungary printed the highest denomination ever created in 1946. It printed a bank note worth 100 quintillion pengoes. A hundred quintillion looks like this: 100,000,000,000,000,000,000 and was worth US $0.20.[17]
- In 2015, Greece froze all domestic bank accounts and allowed people to withdraw a maximum of 60 Euros per day.[18]
- Most of the money in the world today is fiat money or money that is not backed by gold or other metals. The term "fiat" comes from the Latin for "let it be done.[19]" It is money that is accepted simply because a government declares it official money.
- The British pound is the oldest fiat currency in existence at 317 years. The pound was originally defined as 12 oz. of silver. It's now worth less than 0.5% of its original value. In other words, the most

---

[16] https://ideas.oakridgeinvest.com/new-blog-stream/1930-stock-market
[17] https://en.wikipedia.org/wiki/Hungarian_peng%C5%91
[18] https://apnews.com/57fcf1f4694a486aa4b7cd43095ae8ee

[19] https://www.investopedia.com/terms/f/fiatmoney.asp

successful long-standing currency in existence has lost 99.5% of its value.[20]

A SHORT STORY ABOUT MONEY

Kublai Khan was a man way ahead of his time. It was the 13th century and as the Chinese emperor, he had a problem. His China at the time was divided into different regions, many of which issued their own coins. This made it difficult to trade within the empire so Kublai Khan issued a decree that money in China would take the form of paper[21]. With this new law, Kublai Khan changed the perception of what money could be and showed that as long as there was faith that the value of the paper was honored, it could be used as a store of wealth and be used to buy and exchange goods and services.

Today, most money isn't in the form of bills or coins. It is information held in computers at businesses and banks. There is more of that type of money than physical cash and coins. More and more we are paying with checks, credit cards and wire transfers. Prior to cryptocurrencies, we did not have much choice if the bank holding our money closed down unexpectedly. Think about that for a second. Most people think that their money is safe in their bank. They don't give a second thought about not being able to get their money out of their account. Some people keep some extra cash in a safe while others buy gold or silver as a backup, but most of us just trust

---

[20] https://twitter.com/GoldTelegraph_/status/1092449468031524866
[21] https://www.britannica.com/biography/Kublai-Khan

that their money will always be safe in their banks.

Sometimes there have been factors that have caused governments to have to print more money. The printing of new money causes the value of your money to become devalued since there is now more of it in circulation. But there is another bigger problem. In a financial crisis, banks can close their doors unexpectedly. Imagine not being able to go to your bank or ATM and withdraw your money!

DEBT AND MONEY

According to an article from CNBC that ran July of 2018, the global debt climbed to $247 trillion in the first quarter of 2018. This is the total amount of debt in the world including that accumulated by governments, corporations and households combined. Of that amount, the non-financial sector accounted for $186 trillion. The Institute of International Finance reported that the GDP ratio has exceeded 318%.

How much money is there in the world? A market watch report recently stated that the total value of all world money is about 90.4 trillion dollars in fiat currency[22] This included coins, banknotes, money market accounts, as well as saving, checking and time deposits.

---

[22] https://www.marketwatch.com/story/this-is-how-much-money-exists-in-the-entire-world-in-one-chart-2015-12-18

By comparison, the entire cryptocurrency market cap as of January 2019 was 131.7 Billion dollars.[23] Not much when compared to Fiat or even gold. This new asset class of cryptocurrencies has a long way to go to catch up but remember that Bitcoin has only been around 10 years. It's going to be very interesting to see what happens to all of the cryptocurrencies in the next couple of years.

Some cryptocurrencies will undoubtedly grow and as with all new technologies, there will be consolidation and some will ultimately fail. Remember all the companies that came out with computers in the 1980s. How many are still around today?

Either way, this book will help you to understand and navigate through this new technological wave.

The graph below is from the visualcapitalist.com website[24] and it breaks down $63 trillion of world debt by country, as well as highlighting each country's debt-to-GDP ratio. The data comes from the IMF and only covers public government debt. It excludes the debt of the country's citizens and businesses, as well as unfunded liabilities which are not yet technically incurred yet.

---

[23] https://coinmarketcap.com/

[24] https://www.visualcapitalist.com/

Rank	Country	Debt-to-GDP Ratio (2017)
#1	Japan	237.6%
#2	Greece	181.8%
#3	Lebanon	146.8%
#4	Italy	131.8%
#5	Portugal	125.7%
#6	Sudan	121.6%
#7	Singapore	111.1%
#8	United States	105.2%
#9	Belgium	103.4%
#10	Egypt	103.0%

Japan and Greece are the most indebted countries in the world, with debt-to-GDP ratios of 237.6% and 181.8% respectively. Meanwhile, the United States sits in the #8 spot with a 105.2% ratio and recent Treasury estimates putting the national debt at $22 trillion. Seven of the fifteen countries with the most total debt are European. Together, excluding Russia, the European continent holds over 26% of total world debt. Combining the debt of the United States, Japan and Europe together accounts for 75% of the total global debt.

The reason that these numbers are so important is that we need to understand that the financial problems we are facing in America are happening all over the world. What is also concerning is the fact that none of these countries seem to be interested in trying to bring down these debts. These amounts cannot be sustained forever.

In 2008, we narrowly averted a dangerous financial crisis when the American banking industry began to fail. The United States government had to take some drastic steps to make save the country from a massive catastrophic event that would have crippled the country and then quickly affect the rest of the world.

THE UNBANKED

While more than two-thirds of the adult population has access to banks, 1.7 billion adults still remain unbanked. The unbanked population is predominantly found in developing countries such as Bangladesh, China, India, much of Latin America, Nigeria and Pakistan. By demographics, more than half of those unbanked are women and come from the poorest 40% of households within their country. Having some sort of banking account is the first step in helping the unbanked. An account that allows a person to send and receive and store money gives them access to other financial services. Ensuring that people worldwide can have access to a transaction account is the focus of the World Bank Group's Universal Financial Access 2020 initiative[25].

1.7 Billion

Unbanked adults worldwide (2017)

1 Billion

Unbanked adults that the WBG has committed to enable to be reached

34 Partners

Made commitments towards th goal

[25] By Jeff Ogden (W163) - Own work, based on figures from the Wikipedia:List of countries by number of Internet users article in the English Wikipedia, which is in turn based on figures from the International Telecommunications Union (ITU) for 2010 (updated to use figures for 2012 on 28 June 2013) (updated to 2016 on 5 Jan 2019).The source code of this SVG is valid.This W3C-unspecified vector image was created with a text editor.This vector image includes elements that have been taken or adapted from this: BlankMap-World6.svg., CC BY-SA 3.0, https://commons.wikimedia.org/w/index.php?curid=19202338

The UFA goal is that by 2020, adults, who currently aren't part of a formal financial system, will be able to have access to an account they can use to store money, send and receive payments and have the basic building block to manage their financial lives.

THE WORLD BANK GROUP

The World Bank and IFC has committed to enabling 1 billion people to gain access to a transaction account through targeted interventions. Over 34 partners have pledged commitments toward achieving universal financial access.

With two-thirds of this unbanked population having access to a mobile phone, the door is opening to mobile banking services as long as mobile access can be combined with well-developed payments system, infrastructure, regulations and consumer protection safeguards. Tailoring services to counter barriers for specific populations, including those with low literacy and numeracy skills, is likely to improve access further.

While this was happening, an anonymous person or persons named Satoshi Nakamoto published a white paper to a group of computer coders on an email list in which he described a software protocol for a digital cash system that used an underlying digital cryptocurrency called Bitcoin. This cryptocurrency enabled people to do transactions from person to person without having to rely on a third party. At the time, nobody realized that this document would soon change the world in a very profound way.

CURRENCY IS A TOOL OF TRADE

What is money? Why do we need it? How much money is there in the world? All good questions. I never really thought much about these questions until my granddaughter asked me one day, "Pops, what is money?" I immediately said money is what you use to buy things. That answer seemed to work for a 4-year-old but I knew that it was only a matter of time before she asked me more difficult questions about money so I started to do a little research about money and here is what I came up with.

According to Wikipedia, "Money is any item or verifiable record that is generally accepted as payment for goods and services and repayment of debts in a particular country or socio-economic context"[26]. Does a cryptocurrency like Bitcoin fit this description? Let's take a look.

Wikipedia's definition went on to say that money has to have several main functions to be considered money.

Those functions are:

- a medium of exchange
- a unit of account
- a store of value

Does a cryptocurrency like Bitcoin act as a medium of exchange and a unit of account and a store of value? In my

---

[26] https://en.wikipedia.org/wiki/Money

opinion, it certainly does. Bitcoin is bought and sold every day all over the world and many people have been holding Bitcoin in their wallets much like people hold gold as a way of storing value and some people even hold Bitcoin in their IRAs!

In addition, any item or verifiable record that fulfills these functions can be considered as money.

- Fungibility: its individual units must be capable of mutual substitution (i.e., interchangeability).
- Durability: it should be able to withstand repeated use.
- Portability: it can be easily carried and transported.
- Cognizability: its value must be easily identified.
- Stability of value: its value should not fluctuate.

As we will see later on, Bitcoin meets many of the functions of a currency although we will also see that it has some other features that sometimes make it act like an asset.

SO HOW IS MONEY CREATED?

For the most part, money is created by one of two ways:

- Legal tender by a central bank
- Bank money by private banks

Legal tender is the money created by a central bank when they mint coins or print paper banknotes.

Bank money is the money created by private banks through the recording of their loans as deposits of clients borrowing or taking out loans. Bank money is created as electronic money, basically just entries in a banks ledger. When we purchase something with our credit cards, we are just making electronic changes to the banks' ledgers.

The majority of money in most countries is created as bank money by commercial banks making loans. These banks do not depend on a central bank for their money, they just create new loans and deposits making money out of thin air. **Now you know why you want to own a bank!**

I think that is important that we also talk a little bit about the different types of money that we use. This can help us understand where we've come from and also help us understand some of the controversies about money and cryptocurrencies and how they differ.

TYPES OF MONEY

Representative - Representative money is money that consists of either coins, paper money or other physical paper such as certificates that can be exchanged for a fixed quantity of a commodity such as gold or silver. Representative money represents something of value but has little or no intrinsic value on its own. The value of representative money has a direct and fixed relationship to the commodity that backs it, while not being composed of that commodity. American dollars were once a representative type of money that was backed by gold and silver. In 1971, President Nixon got America off the gold standard. The American dollar then became fiat currency that was no longer backed by gold and silver but by the trust in the American government.

This dollar bill has the words "United States Note" at the top of the bill instead of "Federal Reserve Note" that we see on US currency today. Notice that the words "Will Pay to the Bearer on Demand" beneath the image of George Washington. You could go into any bank and receive gold or silver for your note until 1933.

Fiat - Fiat money or fiat currency is money whose value is not derived from any intrinsic value. It cannot be converted into a valuable commodity (such as gold). Instead, it has value only by government order (fiat). Usually, the government declares and then creates fiat currency. In the United States, it is the Federal Reserve System that controls and determine the creation of new money and the United States Mint that is in charge of creating coins while the Bureau of Engraving and Printing creates the paper money.

Coinage - Coinage is money that uses non-precious metals as coins. Early civilizations first used metals for their coins. These metals were mined, weighed and stamped into coins. The weighing of the coins assured the holders of the coins that they were of a specific weight and therefore of a specific value. The value is the metal itself. Early popular metals used for coinage were silver, gold and bronze. Currently, the US uses copper-plated zinc coins for pennies and copper nickel-plated metals for all other coins.

Electronic or digital - Now that we have a good understanding of the various types of money and how they are used, we can talk about this new form of electronic or digital money. This new class of money is sometimes referred to as cryptocurrency and the cryptocurrency that started it all is a cryptocurrency named Bitcoin.

THE GODFATHER – BITCOIN

Until now, if a person had to send or transfer money, they would have to use a trusted third party such as a bank or companies such as MoneyGram or Western Union to facilitate the transfer. There are obviously problems that can come up when having to transfer money in this way. There might be limitations on the amount of money that can be sent as is the case with MoneyGram and Western Union. If a person does not have an account at a bank, it becomes difficult to send or receive money. Sometimes there are delays if the money has to be routed through various banks before getting to its final destination.

Bitcoin has changed all that. Now money can be sent directly to a person regardless of their having a bank account. If you have a Bitcoin wallet with some Bitcoins, you can send it directly to anyone else who has a Bitcoin wallet. All you need is their wallet's public address.

David Sacks, the founder of PayPal in a CNBC interview stated, " In its purest form, currency is confidence. It's a network effect around an agreed-upon medium of exchange that has some promise of scarcity. Bitcoin enforces its scarcity through a combination of cryptography and economic incentives("crypto-economics"). A lot of people find that more comforting than relying on the good faith of a government. In math we trust."[27]

Fiat Inflation around the world

I'm often asked if Bitcoin is a real coin? My answer is that it's real in the sense that it exists, but it is not a physical coin like a dollar bill. Bitcoin is a digital currency that exists as ones and zeros. Bitcoins are not printed or minted like US Dollars or Euros or Yen. You can't physically touch them but you can print out a representative of them in the form of their public

---

[27] https://www.cnbc.com/2017/08/14/david-sacks-cryptocurrency-interview.html

address. Bitcoins and many other cryptocurrencies are created or "mined" by "nodes" (computers) and exist as a digital number on a computer ledger.

The computers that mine these cryptocurrencies are connected all over the world and operate 24 hours a day, 7 days a week competing to solve complex mathematical equations. The computer that solves the mathematical problem first gets rewarded in Bitcoins. The amount of Bitcoins rewarded gets reduced by half every four years until all 21 million Bitcoins have been created or "mined".

By mining, the total Bitcoins available slowly and steadily increases and is added to the available pool of Bitcoins in circulation. The Bitcoin software protocol has been designed to create only 21 million Bitcoins. As of January 2019, over 17 million Bitcoins or 85% of the total number of Bitcoins have been mined. Sometime in 2040, the last Bitcoins will be mined and all 21 million Bitcoins will be in circulation.

When we talk about Bitcoin, we are actually talking about two things: a decentralized network (Blockchain) and the actual coin (Bitcoin). A Bitcoin can be sent electronically from one user to another anywhere in the world without passing through a central authority, such as a bank or payment gateway. A Bitcoin can be divided out to eight decimal places meaning you can send someone 0.00000001 of a Bitcoin. This smallest fraction of a Bitcoin is referred to as a Satoshi, after the anonymous creator of Bitcoin.

Bitcoin is also a protocol, a distributed network that maintains a ledger of balances of Bitcoin the coin. The Bitcoin protocol enables payments to be sent between users without passing through a central authority, such as a bank or payment gateway. This is what is commonly called the Blockchain.

The Bitcoin Blockchain is decentralized. That means that the Blockchain does not exist in just one central computer but on computers all over the world. In addition, anyone can download the Bitcoin software which is in the public domain and install it on their computer. By running the software, your computer acts as a node that can verify transactions on the Bitcoin Blockchain. Because of the way that the verification process works, it is not possible for someone to take over the network, steal funds, create more Bitcoins or change the software.

IS BITCOIN AN ASSET, A CURRENCY OR A COMMODITY?

Bitcoins and other cryptocurrencies are sometimes referred to or considered to be either an asset or security, a currency or a commodity. For someone wanting to send money to their family without incurring large transfer fees, Bitcoin acts as a currency. For an investor purchasing crypto coins to diversify their portfolio, Bitcoin acts as a commodity or security. For someone buying some Bitcoin to put in their IRA, it may be acting as a commodity. The good news is that it is legal to own Bitcoin and use it in all of these ways.

There is still some confusion and sometimes not everyone agrees on how to categorize Bitcoin and some of the other cryptocurrencies. The US. Commodities Futures Trading Commission (CFTC) recently declared cryptocurrencies to be a commodity, which means it intends to regulate them in the same way as physical commodities are regulated.

The IRS requires that any capital gains from the sale of cryptocurrencies be reported on your individual tax return.

If a cryptocurrency is termed a security, then it falls under the jurisdiction of the Securities and Exchange Commission (SEC). There are three elements that determine if an asset a security.

1. Can it be exchanged for some value?
2. Does it involve some element of risk in return for profit?
3. Can it be tradable by others?

The Howey test was created by the United States Supreme Court in 1946 as a quick and easy way to determine whether a transaction is a valid "investment contract".[28]

If you plan on purchasing cryptocurrencies whether for long term holding or short term trading, you need to be aware of the

---

[28] https://en.wikipedia.org/wiki/SEC_v._W._J._Howey_Co.

tax consequences. This is exactly what the IRS has to say about cryptocurrencies. This notice comes directly from their website.

Notice 2014-21

SECTION 1. PURPOSE

This notice describes how existing general tax principles apply to transactions using virtual currency. The notice provides this guidance in the form of answers to frequently asked questions.

SECTION 2. BACKGROUND

The Internal Revenue Service (IRS) is aware that "virtual currency" may be used to pay for goods or services, or held for investment. Virtual currency is a digital representation of value that functions as a medium of exchange, a unit of account and /or a store of value. In some environments, it operates like "real" currency -- i.e., the coin and paper money of the United States or of any other country that is designated as legal tender, circulates and is customarily used and accepted as a medium of exchange in the country of issuance -- but it does not have legal tender status in any jurisdiction. Virtual currency that has an equivalent value in real currency, or that acts as a substitute for real currency, is referred to as "convertible" virtual currency. Bitcoin is one example of a convertible virtual currency. Bitcoin can be digitally traded between users and can be purchased for, or exchanged into, U.S. dollars, Euros and other real or virtual currencies. For a more comprehensive description of convertible virtual currencies to date, see Financial Crimes Enforcement Network (FinCEN) Guidance on the Application of FinCEN's Regulations to Persons Administering, Exchanging, or Using Virtual Currencies (FIN-2013-G001, March 18, 2013).

SECTION 3. SCOPE

In general, the sale or exchange of convertible virtual currency, or the use of convertible virtual currency to pay for goods or services in a real-world economy transaction, has tax consequences that may result in a tax liability. This notice addresses only the U.S. federal tax consequences of transactions in, or transactions that use, convertible virtual currency and the term "virtual currency" as used in Section 4 refers only to convertible virtual currency. No inference should be drawn with respect to virtual currencies not described in this notice. The Treasury Department and the IRS recognize that there may be other questions regarding the tax consequences of virtual currency not addressed in this notice that warrants consideration. Therefore, the Treasury Department and the IRS request comments from the public regarding other types or aspects of virtual currency transactions that should be addressed in future guidance.[29]

WHAT DOES THIS MEAN FOR YOU?

A few things to note about the IRS's position on cryptocurrencies. For federal tax purposes, a cryptocurrency is treated as property so general tax principles applicable to property transactions apply to all transactions using cryptocurrencies. This is important to note. A taxpayer who receives a cryptocurrency as payment for goods or services must, in computing gross income, include the fair market value of the virtual currency calculated in U.S. dollars, as of the date that the virtual currency was received. You will run into problems when it comes time to report your taxes if you fail to calculate and keep track of the values. This includes anyone who "mines" cryptocurrencies. You must report what the fair market value of the coins mined was at the time you received or mined the coins.

All of this means that if you are holding or trading or mining or selling cryptocurrencies, it would be a good idea that you consult with your tax advisor and make sure that you are not going to run afoul of the IRS. I use cointracking software to track all of my purchases and sales. It provides me with all sorts of reports including the ones that my accountant needs.

---

[29] https://www.irs.gov/irb/2014-16_IRB#NOT-2014-21

Finally, I think that we need to put Bitcoin in perspective when compared to the global money supply. While Bitcoin's market cap is impressive, it has a long way to go before it reaches the likes of Google, Amazon and Apple. But remember that Bitcoin has only been around 10 years.

The Winklevoss brothers, who are the owners of the Gemini Crypto exchange and are Bitcoin billionaires, feel that Bitcoin has the potential to reach thirty to forty times its current value. At that valuation, Bitcoin's future market cap would be over $5 trillion!

Gold .... $8.2 Trillion

US Dollars in circulation .... $1.5 Trillion

Apple Computer .... $900 Billion

Google .... $816 Billion

Amazon .... $797 Billion

All Cryptocurrencies .... $267 Billion

Bitcoin .... $185 Billion

Chapter 3. The Blockchain

What is the Blockchain? You hear that word almost as much as you hear the word Bitcoin and with good reason. Before Blockchain, if you had to make a major financial transaction like buying a car or a house or even send someone large amounts of money, you had to go through a third party intermediary. Blockchain eliminates that and allows people to transact directly. The reason that Bitcoin exists is because of the Blockchain and the reason that the Blockchain exists is because of Bitcoin. In very simple terms, **the Blockchain is nothing more than a large database or ledger**, but the Blockchain is a very special kind of database.

The Bitcoin Blockchain is a persistent, transparent, public and append-only online database. You can add data to this database ledger but you cannot change the data on the ledger therefore it is an "append only" database. Blockchains are cryptographically secured which means that mathematical techniques for encrypting and decrypting used in order to keep the data private when it's transmitted or stored. Blockchains are distributed so there is no central authority that controls the Blockchain. The Blockchain is also tamper resistant, so you cannot alter the data once entered and the data on the Blockchain is time stamped so there is permanent accountability of the time the data was entered. The word Blockchain comes from the fact that you create "blocks" of data of transactions. As these blocks get finalized, some additional information is added to the blocks before they get compressed by a process called "hashing". Once the block is hashed, it gets added to the previous block of data creating a chain of blocks or a "Blockchain".

THE VALUE OF BLOCKCHAINS

Before Blockchains, I could send you a phone or music file but I still retained the original. it was almost impossible to prove and track ownership of these types of digital files. More importantly, it was impossible for me to send you money digitally without going through a middleman such as a bank or a service like MoneyGram or Western Union.

Blockchain technology created a whole new digital asset class that allowed for the safe sending of digital assets. Using Blockchain, we can now prove ownership of these digital assets in a decentralized way without the need for an intermediary or third party.

To quote Vitalik Buterin, the inventor of Ethereum,
"Blockchain solves the problem of manipulation. When I speak about it in the West, people say they trust Google, Facebook, or their banks. But the rest of the world doesn't trust organizations and corporations that much - I mean Africa, India, Eastern Europe, or Russia. It's not about the places

where people are really rich. Blockchain's opportunities are the highest in the countries that haven't reached that level yet."[30]

Most Blockchains are designed to be decentralized. Decentralization means that there is not just one computer holding all the blocks, but a network of nodes (computers) all over the world operating in a peer to peer basis checking and verifying transactions. This decentralization makes it very difficult to hack or alter the contents of the Blockchain because there are multiple copies of the Blockchain on computers all over the world. These computers (nodes) all have to agree on the number and sequence of the transactions being added to a block. In other words, they have to be in consensus. Any node who has transactions that disagree with the rest of the nodes' transactions gets rejected. This makes it extremely hard for someone to try to hack the Blockchain.

TYPES OF BLOCKCHAINS

Public - A public Blockchain means that it is open to the public for viewing. The first public Blockchain was the Bitcoin Blockchain invented by Satoshi Nakamoto in 2008 and served as the transaction ledger for the cryptocurrency Bitcoin. The Bitcoin Blockchain made it possible to solve the double-spending problem of cryptocurrencies without the need for a trusted authority or central server. Because the Bitcoin Blockchain is public and transparent, no one is in charge and

---

[30] https://www.cryptoclothesline.com/blog-posts/Blockchain-solves-the-problem-of-manipulation/

anyone can participate in the reading and auditing the Blockchain but no one can alter the Blockchain once transactions are recorded on it. Anyone can review all the transactions at any given point of time on it. I highly recommend that you download and read Satoshi Nakamoto's white paper on Bitcoin. It is a very fascinating document and may help you in understanding and the thinking and the reasoning Satoshi had behind Bitcoin. You can download it at this URL address. (https://cryptocurrencyinfo.today/Bitcoin-white-paper-satoshi-nakamoto/)

Private - A private Blockchain has permissions that only participants with the correct credentials can use or access. Access is restricted and someone cannot use a private Blockchain unless invited by the Blockchain's network administrators. Also, users of a private Blockchain cannot read/write or audit the Blockchain unless they have permission to do so. In a private Blockchain, a consensus is achieved by a central authority or owner who might be a single entity or a company. The owner of the Blockchain can override, add and delete transactions on a Blockchain if needed. Some people consider private Blockchains to be nothing more than a centralized ledger or database that uses cryptography to secure it on the Blockchain but private Blockchains have some key advantages over public Blockchains. For one, private Blockchains are typically faster and cheaper than public Blockchains because they don't require as much work to reach a consensus, meaning less need for many nodes and typically the need for less computing power, but there are some disadvantages to private Blockchains. Some people consider them to be much less secure compared to public Blockchains because they can be edited and written or read by whoever has control of them. Others feel that they go against the spirit of having an open-source public ledger like Bitcoin's Blockchain.

Consortium - This type of Blockchain tries to remove the problem of having one entity control when using private Blockchains. In a consortium, you have several entities or companies or individuals that come together and make decisions for the best benefit of the entire network. A consortium Blockchain is often said to be semi-decentralized because while it has permissions, instead of a single organization controlling the Blockchain, a number of companies might each operate a node on the network.

The administrators of a consortium chain restrict users' reading rights as they see fit and only allow a limited set of trusted nodes to execute a consensus protocol. This seems to be the approach that Facebook is planning on using with their Libra coin.

Distributed Ledgers - A distributed ledger is a database that exists across numerous computers or nodes and not in a central location. Having a centralized database offers some potential problems in that there is one one point of failure. Because a distributed ledger is decentralized, it eliminates the need for a central authority or intermediary to process, validate or authenticate transactions. All the files in a distributed ledger are time stamped and given a unique cryptographic signature. All of the participants on the distributed ledger can view all of the records on the ledger and the technology provides a verifiable and auditable history of all the information stored on that ledger.

How Do Blockchain And Distributed Ledgers Differ?

Think of the Blockchain and the distributed ledger in the same way you might think of Pampers and diapers. Pampers are just a brand of diapers, but pampers have become so popular that when you say pampers, people think of diapers. The same with Blockchain and distributed ledger. The Blockchain is just one type of distributed ledger. A key difference to be aware of is that although the Blockchain is comprised of a sequence of blocks on a chain, distributed ledgers do not require or need a chain. It's the removing of the intermediary party from the distributed ledger equation that makes the technology so appealing to many. Unlike the Blockchain, a distributed ledger does not necessarily need to have its data structure in a Blockchain. A distributed ledger is just a type of database that is spread across multiple sites or nodes. In the end, you can say that all Blockchains are distributed ledgers, but not all distributed ledgers are Blockchains.

WHAT IS FORKING?

Forking is a term that is used when a computer project splits into a totally new project. The reasons for wanting to "fork" or split can be anywhere from developers trying to solve problems with the original project to disagreements by the developers as to what new additions should be added to the project. Sometimes the reasons can be resolved and sometimes the differences are so great between the developers to the point that there is no way resolving the differences as to how to move forward with a project.

At that point, the project may come to a standstill until a consensus is reached as to how to move forward. If these issues cannot be solved, a "fork" of the project may be created by some of the developers of the project. At that time, a new version is created and the development of the project can continue with either the new version of the project or a continuation of the old project in addition to the new project. This has happened several times to Bitcoin and Ethereum. That is why you now see Bitcoin Cash, Bitcoin Gold and Bitcoin SV and Ethereum Classic.

Chapter 4. Mining

Mining - The term "mining" refers to computers that use special software to solve complex mathematical problems in hopes of being the first computer that successfully solves the problem. The "miner" gets rewarded by being able to add a block of transactions to the chain. In addition, once a block is mined and solved, the miners are also rewarded with new coins for securing and verifying transactions on that block.

Cryptocurrency miners use specialized hardware to mine coins. In the early days of mining, miners just used their computers CPU processor to mine coins. Anyone with a computer and software was capable of mining. Soon people learned that some of their gaming computers had Graphic Process Unit chips that they could adapt and use for mining. These chips were much faster than their computers CPU chip and would allow miners to process and mine faster. People then figured out that they could chain computers together to get even more processing power. More recently, companies have started to create specialized cards called ASICs. ASICs are created especially for mining. They are very fast and designed to consume less electricity than a normal computer rig but they are also very specialized and can usually only be used to mine a specific crypto. GPUs on the other hand can mine almost any coin but at a slower rate.

There are several factors or metrics that miners use when considering what equipment to get for mining. After determining the coin to be mined, you need to decide the difficulty of the algorithm, the network hash rate and the cost of electricity to produce one coin. The most important of these is and the one that all miners look at is the hash rate-to-power ratio. The higher the hash rate and the lower the power consumption, the more profitable for the miner. It's also important to factor in the cost of the equipment. The higher the initial cost, the longer it will take to recoup upfront expenses so the ideal setup is an inexpensive card that has a low power consumption and a high hash rate. One other factor that influences miners is the popularity of the coin. If the coin's price goes up because of demand or hype and speculation, then more miners join the network trying to mine coins, increasing that coin's hash rate, which increases the difficulty. It becomes harder and less profitable to mine a block and get rewarded.

You also need reliable and cheap electricity to stay profitable while running the mining equipment. That is why you will notice that there are a lot of mining operations in places where you can get cheap electricity.

If you were thinking of trying to mine Bitcoin, you would need to use an ASIC card but unless you have a lot of them, you can forget trying to get even one Bitcoin from mining. If you were thinking of trying to mine one of the many other coins out there, you could use a GPU miner. They are less expensive but you will still run into the same problem of cost of time/equipment/electricity cost vs. the potential payout. The days of having a single computer mining crypto are pretty much over. Large server farms have taken over most mining operations.

TYPES OF MINING

Cloud Mining - When you do cloud mining, you are buying a certain amount of computing power (referred to as hash) from a company that is running computer mining equipment.

These companies or mining contractors provide mining services with performance specified by a contract, often called a "Mining Contract." The contract you purchase will specify a level of mining capacity for a set price for a specific duration. Typically these large mining farms are running hundreds of computers and your participation helps reduce their costs while at the same time receiving a return on your investment.

Pool Mining – Another option for people that want to get into Mining is to join a **Mining Pool**. People that had previously purchased mining equipment soon found that were still not being able to mine coins like they had in the past because others now had faster equipment or because of these powerful new server farms. Miners realized that they were wasting time and electricity competing for a limited amount of blocks and still not receiving any reward for their mining efforts so to try to solve the problem some miners began organizing themselves into groups. These groups could pool their computing power to mine and if successful, they would share in the profits. There are many large mining pools that you can join but as with everything else in crypto, do your research before joining and sending money to anyone.

Hardware Mining – Hardware mining refers to using a computer with special hardware, memory and graphic cards to mine cryptocurrencies. Your computer runs the mining software and tries to solve the complex algorithms. In the early days of Bitcoin, it was possible to mine Bitcoin using something as small as a laptop but those days are gone. Large server farms with hundreds of computers have taken over most of the mining of Bitcoin and other cryptocurrencies so don't waste your time trying to mine Bitcoin or any of the larger cryptocurrencies. Those days are gone.

Chapter 5. Exchanges

Cryptocurrency exchanges are online platforms that allow you to exchange one cryptocurrency for another. Some exchanges allow you to exchange your cryptocurrencies for fiat currencies. Some exchanges act more like a stock exchange while others are more like a currency exchange that you might find at an airport. I've listed the different types of exchanges so that you have a better idea of what services they offer and how you might go about choosing one.

Traditional Cryptocurrency Exchanges - These exchanges act like traditional stock exchanges where buyers and sellers trade cryptocurrencies for other assets, such as conventional fiat money or other digital currencies based on the current market price. These exchanges usually charge a fee for each transaction you make.

Cryptocurrency Brokers - These are website-based exchanges similar to what you might see at a money exchange at an airport. They allow customers to buy and sell cryptocurrencies at a price set by the broker (generally at the market price plus a small premium). Here the exchange is between the buyer or seller and the broker, not between a buyer and seller. Coinbase is an example of this type of exchange.

Direct Trading Platforms - These exchanges offer direct peer-to-peer trading between buyers and sellers. Exchanges of this type do not use a fixed market price when exchanging cryptos. Instead, sellers set their own exchange rate and buyers can find sellers on the platform that meet their required price and form of payment and perform an Over the Counter (OTC) exchange by the agreed upon method. Buyers can also post the price they are willing to buy crypto for and the platform will match the buyer and seller. The benefit of these types of platforms is that they don't require a sometimes long verification process that other types of exchanges require that can slow down the buying and selling process. The downside is that the fees can sometimes be higher than those you would pay when using a more traditional exchange.

Cryptocurrency exchanges are the lifeblood of the cryptocurrency world. Most users initially use an exchange to purchase their Bitcoins or Ethereum, hold their cryptos, trade their cryptos and to monitor prices. Choosing the right exchange can be daunting and there is really no best exchange. It comes down to what you need from an exchange, how familiar you are with cryptocurrencies and where you live. The following are some of the cryptocurrency exchanges that I like and use.

Bittrex - Bittrex is a US-based cryptocurrency exchange that is headquartered in Seattle, Washington. Great for beginners and advanced user, as of March 2019, the Bittrex exchange had over 25 million in daily trading volume. It allows its users to trade over 190+ cryptocurrencies listed on their exchange.

Binance - Binance is one of the most popular exchanges because of its low trading fees and a variety of available crypto currencies. They have become the number one exchange for Bitcoin by volume as of 2019. Users can receive up to 50% off on trading fees, if the transaction uses their coin (BNB).

Poloniex - Poloniex an exchange owned by Circle, a large Goldman-Sachs backed company. Circle also launched USDC which is a US dollar based stable coin. They are based out of Wilmington, Delaware. Because it is based in the US, users must provide full identity verification and many personal details so you will be required to take a picture of your driver's license or passport if you are purchasing cryptocurrencies with a credit card.

Kraken - Kraken is a cryptocurrency exchange based in San Francisco. It launched operations in the US and Canada in 2013. It's the number one exchange by Euro trade volume and pioneered the first verifiable cryptographic proof of reserves audit system. In 2014 it was listed on the Bloomberg Terminal providing Bitcoin pricing. In April 2017, according to reports, Kraken launched fiat funding options to transfer denominated US dollars and government-issued currencies.[31]

---

[31] https://en.wikipedia.org/wiki/Kraken_(company)

Coinbase - Coinbase, based in San Francisco, is the world's largest Bitcoin exchange. It is the exchange that most first time user like because of its easy to use interface. Because it is based in the US, users must provide full identity verification and many personal details so you will be required to take a picture of your driver's license or passport if you are purchasing cryptocurrencies with a credit card.

Changelly - Changelly is an instant cryptocurrency exchange with a trading algorithm that is integrated into the largest cryptocurrency exchange platforms, including Binance, Poloniex and Bittrex. Changelly allows you to exchange cryptocurrencies fast and also buy Bitcoin, Ethereum and Bitcoin Cash for US dollars and Euros. The Changelly service provides one of the best crypto-to-crypto exchange rates and supports over 130 cryptocurrencies. All you need in order to buy from Changelly is a credit or debit card or you can also use any of the cryptocurrencies that they have on their exchange.

Kucoin - Although it is a relatively new addition to the cryptocurrency exchange world, Kucoin has already proven itself and the exchange has been growing ever since its launch in 2017. Since then, the team has launched the Kucoin Bonus Plan, added additional currencies and brought out mobile apps for both Android and iOS. KuCoin, which is Singapore-based, has partnered with the Israel-based payment processing company Simplex to let its users purchase crypto via credit card. Now users can purchase Bitcoin (BTC), Ethereum (ETH),

Ripple (XRP), Bitcoin Cash ABC (BCHABC) and Litecoin (LTC) for both dollars and euros. The service is available in more than 100 countries. I especially like the fact that you can buy Kucoin tokens and stake them. Staking is a great way to increase your holdings of a token. I talk more about it in the terminology chapter.

Robinhood - Robinhood is one of the newer entries into the cryptocurrency arena. The popular stock trading app now also allows you to buy, sell and store cryptos. It's ideal for investors who want to trade stocks, options, exchange-traded funds and cryptocurrency without paying commissions or fees but there is a tradeoff for it being free. You have to wait a few days when moving funds from fiat to crypto and there are not very many bells and whistles on the App. Otherwise, The app is fairly easy to use but more experienced investors may find the range of tradable securities and account options missing but for first time user who want to get their feet wet, its great. I still use it and buy and sell a combination of stocks and cryptos.

Bakkt - Bakkt (pronounced "backed") is the newest kid on the block and is set to launch its Bitcoin futures trading September 23, 2019. The futures contracts will be margined by the Intercontinental Exchange ICE (the parent company of the New York Stock Exchange NYSE). This is a huge event and milestone in the Crypro space. When the New York Stock Exchange decides to get into the cryptocurrency space, you know that its a very big deal. Bakkt will enable consumers and institutions to buy, sell, store and spend digital assets on their global network. Bakkt's investment partners include companies like Microsoft, Boston Consulting Group and Starbucks, along with some of WallStreet's largest investors such as Galaxy Digital, Fortress Investment Group, Susquehanna International Group, Horizons Ventures and Pantera Capital. The entry of Bakkt into the cryptocurrency exchange market is going to impact the entire cryptocurrency market because there is currently approximately 20 trillion dollars worth of investment funds just waiting for a large, regulated and safe exchange where they can buy Bitcoin and access other cryptocurrency markets. The entry of this exchange is certainly going to help boost the entire space which can only be a good thing.

Tip: I use CoinMarketCap.com as a resource. The website not only lists all of the cryptocurrencies in order of ranking by volume but you can sort by tokens or coins and see which ones are going up or down. You can also see a complete list of all exchanges, crypto trends and they even have a cryptocurrency converter in case you want to know how much Ethereum you would get for your Bitcoin.

Remember that some exchanges do not serve all countries and will not work for all traders. You might need to use several exchanges depending on the crypto you are purchasing or trading. I try to always go with the top exchanges that have high transaction volumes and stay away from the smaller exchanges.

Chapter 6. Wallets

Wallet - A wallet is actually just a software program that is used to store, send and receive digital currency. The term wallet is used because it is similar to how you would hold cash in a physical wallet. These digital wallets save your private keys and allow you to send and receive your cryptocurrencies. Most coins will have an official wallet and some coins will have several recommended third-party wallets. In order to use any cryptocurrency, you will need to use some type of cryptocurrency wallet. There are several things to consider when choosing a wallet depending on how you plan to use and store your cryptocurrencies.

There are five main types of wallets: desktop, mobile, web, hardware and cold storage. Let's take a look at the differences between them.

Desktop wallets - Desktop wallets are installed on a desktop computer and provide the user with complete control over the wallet. Desktop wallets enable the user to create a Bitcoin address for sending and receiving the Bitcoins. They also allow the user to store a private key. A few of the more popular desktop wallets are Exodus, Bitcoin Core, Armory, Electrum and Jaxx. Exodus is my personal favorite.

Mobile wallets - Mobile wallets allow you to take your crypto with you as long as you have a smartphone with the right App. Just install the app and create your keys and you are ready to go. Many cryptocurrencies have their own wallet that will only let you keep that crypto but more and more mobile wallets are now coming out that allow you to keep many different cryptos. Some popular wallets are the Edge, Bread and Jaxx wallets.

Web wallets - Web wallets or online wallets allow you to use and transact from anywhere on any browser or mobile phone. Make sure that you choose your web wallet carefully since it stores your private keys online. There are a few web wallets that now allow you to save your private key offline for better security. MyEtherwallet, MEW Connect, Coinbase and Blockchain are popular web wallet providers.

Hardware wallets - Hardware wallets are small devices similar to a USB memory stick or hard drive that allow you to encrypt your private keys. Hardware wallets allow you to store, send and receive transactions when connected to your computer. When not being used, they are disconnected making them a very good safe way of storing your coins. The Ledger Nano and Trezor are some of the more popular hardware wallets

Paper wallets - Paper wallets are considered one of the safest ways to store your private keys since they are not connected in any way to the Internet. These types of wallets are often called cold storage wallets because they are not connected to the Internet. Paper wallets are usually made out of paper, but technically they could also be printed on plastic or any other material that you can print information on. What you print on your paper wallet are your private and public keys, usually in QR form, as well as in their long number cryptographic keys format. I suggest that you make several copies in case there is a problem like it getting damaged or lost and also laminate them to prevent tearing or moisture. Two open-source random address and key generators are bitaddress.org and walletgenerator.net. They use your browser's JavaScript engine, so no keys are sent over the Internet and they are both very easy to use.

Chapter 7. Crypto Terms, Lingo and Slang

Part of learning about cryptocurrencies is learning many new words and terms associated with this new space. As you learn more about cryptocurrencies you will hear many new words, terms and acronyms. I am including many of the more popular ones in the book. You should be aware of them since you will probably encounter them when you read or talk to others about cryptocurrencies.

FUD - Fud is an acronym for fear, uncertainty and doubt. It is a technique often used in the crypto space to cast doubts over a token, a coin, or a crypto ICO. Individuals or organizations that want to drive down the price of certain cryptos will spread Fud and wait till people start selling because of the fud before buying. A basic rule I follow is don't always believe everything you read and hear about cryptocurrencies. Do your research because it just might be fud.

FOMO - is an acronym for fear of missing out. It is very common for newbies new to cryptocurrencies to begin to think that they need to buy or invest in every new coin or token for fear of missing out. The best thing you can do if you start to feel like you have FOMO is to stop and take your time and research before jumping into any crypto investments. You are not going to miss out if you take some time and evaluate before jumping in. As always, never invest more than you are willing to lose.

HODL - This acronym is used when you are holding cryptocurrencies for a long time. The term was created when an early Bitcoin trader posted on an online forum titled " I am Hodling". What he was trying to type was that he was holding and not selling. The typo became popular and other holders thought it was a funny misspelling to mean that they were "holding" because they felt that prices were going to go up.

IoT - This acronym stands for "The Internet of things". It's the concept of extending Internet connectivity beyond conventional computing platforms such as personal computers and mobile devices and into any range of traditionally *"dumb"* or non-Internet-enabled physical devices and everyday objects. Embedded with electronics, Internet connectivity and other forms of hardware (such as sensors), these devices can communicate and interact with others over the Internet and they can be remotely monitored and controlled.[32]

P2P - This acronym stands for peer to peer. In a P2P network, the "peers" are computers that are connected to each other via the Internet. Files and other data can be shared directly between the computers on the network without the need for a central server. In other words, each computer on a P2P network becomes its own file server as well as a client.

---

[32] https://en.wikipedia.org/wiki/Internet_of_things

ERC-20 - This acronym stands for Ethereum Request for Comment and is a technical standard used for smart contracts on the Ethereum Blockchain. The 20 refers to the number that was assigned to the request. ERC-20 defines a common list of rules for Ethereum tokens to follow within the larger Ethereum ecosystem, allowing developers to accurately predict the interaction between tokens. ERC-20 tokens are currently the most popular form of token which is why so many people invest in Ethereum but there are other tokens that work on other Blockchains.

DApps - DApps are an abbreviation for decentralized applications. A DApp application is a standalone computer program that has its code running on a decentralized peer-to-peer network. The program or application's data and records are cryptographically stored in a public, decentralized Blockchain in order to avoid a central point of failure. The Dapp application uses a cryptographic token (a token native to its system) to access and use the application. Any value from using the DApp is paid to the miners or developers of the DApp in the application's tokens. Tron and EOS are very popular crypto platforms and are used for creating DApps. For example, 888tron.com is a DApp gambling site using the Tron Blockchain.

Alt coins - (alternative cryptocurrencies) You will sometimes hear the word Altcoin when talking about cryptocurrencies.

Altcoins are coins that are an alternative to Bitcoin. Many altcoins are just a variant of the Bitcoin and are built using Bitcoin's original open-source protocol with some changes to its underlying code, thereby creating an entirely new coin with a different set of features. Litecoin and Dogecoin are good examples of altcoins that are variants of the Bitcoin code.

There are also other altcoins that aren't derived from Bitcoin's open-source protocol. They have created their own Blockchain and protocol that supports their native currency. Some examples of these include Ethereum, EOS, Ripple, NEO and Waves.

Scam coins - Yes, there are numerous cryptocurrencies that are nothing more than coins created by scam artists preying on newbies. Always make sure you do your research before you buy any new or even low volume coins. I've also seen individuals promoting their own cryptocurrency. Anyone can create their own crypto but will it have a useful purpose? That is the question you need to keep in the back of your mind whenever you are looking at purchasing any cryptocurrency. Some examples of scam coins that you might read about are PhenixCoin, DavorCoin, Onecoin and AmericanCoin (AMC). Others are always popping up on the Internet, so be careful and always do your homework before buying any new coins.

CASE STUDY:

BitConnect - You might also have heard of
BitConnect. BitConnect has been one of the largest if
not the largest cryptocurrency scam recently. It's an
important piece of cryptocurrency history that everyone
should be aware of so that they do not fall into a similar
situation. Bitconnect started with an ICO in late 2016
and, at its peak, had a market cap of over $2.6 billion
with its BCC coin valued at over $400 dollars. The
scam worked by promising people that they could
deposit Bitcoin and then lend it back out at an
incredible interest rate. The company promised huge
guaranteed returns with incredible daily payouts and for
a while, they delivered much as Bernie Madoff did with
his investment securities organization.

Bitconnect collapsed when people started to ask more
and more questions and the government started to look
deeper into the company, its principals and its
operations. Cease and desist orders started appearing.
Once that happened, the scheme started to fall apart and
within a few short months, the company collapsed with
their BCC coin dropping over 90% in value. The
exchanges that traded BCC stopped trading the coin and
since everyone had their money in BCC, many of them
got stuck with worthless coins. I can't say it enough, do
your due diligence.

NOTE: One last note on Scam Coins - A great website that you should check out is HoweyCoins (https://www.howeycoins.com). HoweyCoins is a scam website set up by the U.S. Securities and Exchange Commission (SEC) to teach people the dangers of virtual currency investment scams. The website has all characteristics of a real site including a white paper, ICO, endorsements and a team. Check it out. You will see why it is so easy for someone to fall prey to these types of scams.

Tokens - The main difference between altcoins and tokens is their use. Tokens do not exist on their own. Tokens require another platform such as Ethereum to exist and operate. Also, tokens provide a way to define a protocol and also to fund the operating expenses required to host the tokens as a service. In other words, tokens are built on top of the Blockchain. One of the most significant tokens is called ERC-20, which has emerged as the technical standard used for all smart contracts on the Ethereum Blockchain for token implementation.

Other examples of tokens that have their own Blockchain are NEO and Waves. Sometimes people use the term "coin" to refer to what other people call "tokens" and "token" to refer to what others call "coins". Some people will use either name to refer to all the digital assets currently available. However, there are very big differences between crypto coins and crypto tokens, so it's important you know what they are! Altcoins are separate currencies with their own separate Blockchain. Tokens operating on top of their own Blockchain allows them to the creation of decentralized applications. A token can fulfill either one or more of the following functions:

- A currency used as a payment system between parties
- A digital asset
- A means for the accounting of transactions.
- A share or stake in a specific company.
- A way of preventing attacks on a network.
- Payment for using a particular system

We can break down tokens into various types.

Asset/security tokens - These types of tokens represent shares of a business. They differ from equity tokens in that there is no ownership in the underlying asset or company.

As mentioned in Chapter 2, if a cryptocurrency is termed a security, it then it falls under the jurisdiction of the Securities and Exchange Commission (SEC). There are three elements that determine if an asset is a security.

- Can it be exchanged for some value?
- Does it involve some element of risk in return for profit?
- Can it be tradable by others?

Payment tokens - Payment tokens are true cryptocurrencies in that they have their own Blockchain and were primarily designed to be used as a payment mechanism. They are used to make purchases, sales and other financial transactions, as well as provide many of the same functions as fiat currencies. Bitcoin, Monero and Ethereum are examples of payment tokens.

Equity tokens - Equity Tokens are tokens that act as a traditional stock asset. The equity tokens represent ownership in a company's assets and take their value from the success or failure of the company.

Utility tokens - The Merriam-Webster dictionary defines a utility token as "A digital token of cryptocurrency that is issued in order to fund development of the cryptocurrency and that can be later used to purchase a good or service offered by the issuer of the cryptocurrency"[33]

The state of Wyoming is the first elected body in the world to define a utility token as a new type of asset class different from a security or commodity. Wyoming's Utility Token bill is designed to exempt specific cryptocurrencies from state money transmission laws and is the first law of its kind to legally define the way in which specific types of crypto tokens are treated by regulatory bodies if they meet certain requirements.

---

[33] https://www.merriam-webster.com/dictionary/utility%20token

In order to meet these requirements, the token may not be offered as an investment and must be a vehicle for exchange as a utility token.

Non-fungible tokens - Non-fungible tokens (NFT's) are tokens that are unique. They are different from fungible tokens such as Bitcoin or Ethereum and the vast majority of cryptos in that fungible tokens are interchangeable in the same way dollar bills are interchangeable. One dollar bill is the same as any other dollar bill. There is nothing special about any specific dollar bill and they are all worth the same amount, a dollar.

Fungible tokens like Bitcoin are divisible. You can send a fraction of one just like you can with cash. You can pay someone with a $10 bill and get back change. You can also pay someone with one Bitcoin and get some Bitcoin back. On the other hand, non-fungible ERC-721 tokens cannot be divided and must be bought or sold whole. Non-fungible tokens are used to represent unique and individual items. An individual piece of property, an antique clock, a piece of art, baseball cards, can all be represented by non-fungible tokens. Think of an airline ticket. Each ticket is unique in that it is from a certain airline that can only be used on a certain date and time and is unique to a certain seat. There is no other ticket like that one. NFT's are a great solution for tracking, recording and identifying birth certificates, academic credentials and real estate properties.

Hash Rate - The term "hash rate" refers to the speed at which a computer is performing calculations in trying to solve a proof of work algorithm such as Bitcoin's. The higher and faster a computer's hash rate, the better its chances are of solving the algorithm and getting the next block of transactions and coins.

Proof of stake (PoS) - The Proof of Stake algorithm is an alternative algorithm for cryptocurrencies that allows holders of a coin to validate transactions according to how many coins they hold. The owners of certain cryptocurrencies can receive transaction fees for staking their coins. While their coins are "staked", they cannot be used, sold or traded. The more coins you stake, the more staking power you have and the more transaction fees you receive. Proof of Stake cryptocurrencies achieve consensus by the number of computers that are "staking" their coin.

Proof of work (PoW) - Proof of Work is a computer algorithm that Bitcoin and other cryptocurrencies use to confirm transactions and produce new blocks of data that are then added to the chain. These computers get rewards by solving a complex mathematical problem by a process called "Mining". With the PoW protocol, the miners compete against each other to be the first to solve the problem. If they successfully solve the mathematical problem, they get to add the next block of transactions to the chain and get rewarded with new Bitcoins and fees from transactions that they record. This chaining of blocks is how Blockchain got its name.

Staking - Staking in the cryptocurrency world is similar to depositing your money into a bank CD. With a CD, your money is held for a certain period of time by the bank in return for a set interest payment you receive at the end of the term. Cryptocurrency staking is similar in that you purchase crypto coins and keep or hold them in a special cryptocurrency wallet where they are "staked" or held and used by the network for validating transactions. As long as you keep your crypto "staked" in the wallet, you are rewarded with additional crypto. The more coins you have staked and the longer you hold your coins in your wallet, the higher the number of coins you receive. For example, staking the cryptocurrency NEO lets you generate GAS, which is NEO's internal currency. A GAS fee is charged whenever someone creates or changes an asset on the NEO Blockchain. GAS pays for each action and is then distributed to NEO stakers proportionately. The more NEO you have staked, the more GAS you'll earn with each payment. I like NEO because you can stake it on an exchange or a wallet and can earn GAS even when not connected to the Internet.

Decentralized - When talking about cryptocurrencies, you will hear the word decentralized over and over. In a centralized network, your computer is connected to a server someplace. When you access Amazon, you are connecting to one of their servers. All servers are centralized. In a decentralized Internet, you are both the client and the server. Your computer serves out files and is also a client accessing data on the network. This is also called a peer to peer network. On a peer-to-peer sharing system, a file on your computer can be sent directly to the recipient's computer without any intermediary. When talking about cryptocurrencies, we mean that each person controls their own funds and can send them to anyone in a decentralized manner without a central authority.

Private/public key - When you create a cryptocurrency wallet, your wallet generates a public and a private key. These keys work together. The public key is your wallets public address. The private key is also known as a secret key. When you receive funds to your public address, it gets encrypted and the only way to decrypt it is to use your private key to access those funds. The best way to think about wallets is that wallets store both keys but its the private key which gives you access to your public key and your money.

> **NOTE**: Something to know about your cryptocurrencies is that when someone sends some amount to your public key, it is being recorded on the Blockchain and it is not really going into your wallet, it just appears that way. As long as you have your private key and know the public address that was used to receive your crypto, you can always access your funds. Remember, you only use and share your public key and never share your private key. Doing so will allow people to access and retrieve your money. You also need to make doubly sure that you have saved and backed up your private key and stored it in several

places so that you always have access to them if you need them.

ICO's (initial coin offerings) - An ICO, or initial coin offering, is a mechanism used to raise funds for new cryptocurrency projects. For example, in 2014, the Ethereum ICO raised $18 million in Bitcoin or the equivalent of 40 cents per ether. Ethereum reached a high of $1,432.88 on January 13, 2018[34]. As of August 2019, Ethereum is now trading above $212 with a market cap of over $22 billion.[35]

Protocol - Blocks are linked using a specific protocol. A protocol is a software program which forms the backbone of the network. There are many different Blockchain protocols and they depend on the specific cryptocurrency project. Different protocols were designed because of differing objectives or use cases needed for each Blockchain. For example, Bitcoin was primarily designed for executing peer to peer payment transactions on a decentralized network and so the protocol was designed to accommodate those transactions. Ethereum was developed to be more focused on providing a Blockchain platform where distributed apps (DApps) could be developed using smart contracts so a new and different protocol was created that added additional functionality to the Etereum Blockchain.

---

[34] https://coinmarketcap.com/currencies/ethereum/historical-data/
[35] https://coinmarketcap.com/currencies/ethereum/

Node - A node is a device on a network that is connected to the Internet. The node is able to send, receive and /or forward data. While the computer is the most common node, modems, switches, hubs, bridges, servers and even printers can act as nodes. The role of a node is to support the network by maintaining a copy of a Blockchain and, in some cases, to process transactions. Each cryptocurrency uses its own nodes to maintain the transaction history of that particular token. Owners of nodes that contribute to store and validate transactions have the chance to collect the transaction fees and earn a reward in the underlying cryptocurrency. This use of a computer's resources is known as "mining".

Gas - You may have noticed that sometimes you are asked to enter a gas price when sending ethereum or other ERC-20 tokens. Let's use Ethereum to explain this term. Ethereum is a network and a Blockchain. Ether (ETH) is the fuel for that network. Whenever you send tokens or interact with a smart contract, or send Ethereum on the Blockchain, you must pay miners for the work they are providing. If you think about it, it makes sense that the miners get rewarded for adding transactions to the Blockchain. These miners prioritize transactions and then enter the transactions with the highest mining fees first. The miners are free to ignore transactions whose gas price limit is too low. Also, the more complex the commands are that are needed to execute a contract the more gas (and Ether) you will need to pay.

That payment is calculated in gas and gas is paid in Ethereum so gas is nothing more than a unit of measure used to calculate the fees that need to be paid to the network.

Atomic swaps - Atomic swaps enable people to directly trade different types of cryptocurrencies directly with one another in a peer to peer or wallet-to-wallet manner without going through a third-party exchange. They accomplish the swap by using a smart contract. The smart contract allows each party to swap their coins by using a shared secret key while keeping their own private key separate during the swap process. During this process, the parties doing the exchange continue to have full control and ownership of their private keys until the swap is complete. Atomic swaps require both parties to acknowledge receipt of funds within a specified timeframe. If one of the involved parties fails to confirm the transaction within the specified timeframe, then the entire transaction is voided and funds are not exchanged.

Sharding - Sharding is a way of divvying up a piece of data in a transaction to each node on a Blockchain instead of every node having the entire information for every block. These pieces of data are on separate servers so no one server has all the information. This spreading out of the data helps to spread the load. This makes the Blockchain more efficient and more scalable. Because these nodes do not have the entire Blockchain, sharding only works with proof of stake consensus cryptocurrencies such as Dash and Neo.

Off-chain transactions - Off-chain transactions are transactions that happen between two or more parties outside of the Blockchain. Because they happen outside of the Blockchain, they are cheaper, faster and offer more privacy. They are usually cheaper because there is no fee due to there being no third party verifying the transaction. They are faster since you are not waiting for nodes to verify the transaction. They offer more privacy because the transaction is not on the Blockchain.

White paper - A white paper is the document that all ICO's issue when explaining the purpose or reason for starting their project. The ICO's white paper should explain their entire business plan including who they are, their team, what they plan to do, what the problem is that their ICO will solve and a roadmap of how they plan on implementing the project. It should also include the future plans for the project and how the ICO is to be structured financially and how investors will be compensated.

> **NOTE**: Only after reading through a cryptocurrency project's white paper, should you proceed and investigate it further. I cannot stress enough the importance of taking your time and doing your due diligence to determine if the project is worth your time and money as an investment. Determine if the project/idea/service needs to be done on the Blockchain. Does it also need a new cryptocurrency for

it to work? Not all projects need to be on the Blockchain or have their own cryptocurrency. Are there already better solutions/companies already doing the same thing? Remember this as you evaluate your opportunities and as always, never invest more than you are willing to lose. You don't want to be losing sleep over investing in an investment.

Chapter 8. Smart Contracts

According to Wikipedia, "A smart contract is a computer protocol intended to digitally facilitate, verify, or enforce the negotiation or performance of a contract. Smart contracts allow the performance of credible transactions without third parties. These transactions are trackable and irreversible"[36]. That definition while accurate, does not fully explain the implications that smart contracts are going to have in society as they become more prolific so let's begin with the origins of a smart contract and what is actually is.

The concept of the smart contract was first thought up by a computer scientist named Nick Szabo. His publication titled *The Idea of Smart Contracts*[37] outlined the concepts and the term back in 1997. Nick proposed that a decentralized ledger could be used for smart contracts, also called self-executing contracts, Blockchain contracts, or digital contracts. In this digital format, contracts could be converted to computer code, stored and replicated on the system and supervised by the network of computers that run the Blockchain. This would also result in ledger feedback such as transferring money and receiving the product or service. Nick was an early cryptocurrency pioneer and even proposed his idea of a cryptocurrency called Bit Gold in 1998, several years before Bitcoin.

---

[36] https://en.wikipedia.org/wiki/Smart_contract
[37] https://nakamotoinstitute.org/the-idea-of-smart-contracts/

First, let's define a contract. In basic terms, a smart contract is a written contract that has been converted into computer code. This code has the ability to self-verify that certain conditions of the contract are met by the use of complex if-then statements. If the statements verify, then the contract is executed. That is the basic function of a smart contract but in real world applications you can start to see how this can be a game changer.

An important and key benefit of smart contracts is that they are tamper resistant once they are executed. No one can go back and alter any of the terms of the contract. Locking in the terms of the contract ensures that a contract will be executed as written with no outside enforcement required.

Once executed, the Blockchain records and enforces the smart contract. Since the smart contract cannot be altered once executed, some feel that is also a potential problem. If there are important factors or conditions that were not included in the contract that should have been, there is no way to modify to contract once it has been initiated. Also, because the contracts get executed when certain conditions are met without human interaction, there is no way of interpreting the intent of the people entering into the contract as is sometimes needed in a normal written contract. These are a few things that you should make sure you consider if contemplating using a smart contract.

Let's take this scenario. Suppose you want to send some Bitcoin to someone. Maybe you want to purchase a product or pay someone for a service such as a haircut or carwash. Cryptocurrencies such as Bitcoin enable you to send the funds without the need of any third parties or intermediaries. But let's make this transaction a bit more complicated. What if we want to purchase a gift but we want to make sure that the gift is delivered on a certain date and time and location before paying for it. Suppose you are ordering a container of flowers from another country to be delivered to your business. You want to make sure that the flowers are delivered not just on time on a specific date but that they have also been kept at a certain temperature while being transported. All of these conditions need to be met before you will pay for the flowers.

This introduces conditions, rules and policies beyond the scope of a simple money transfer that cryptocurrency protocols can handle. A smart contract addresses these types of conditions and allows for these validations to be stored on the Blockchain thus making it easy not only to check if all the conditions were met before releasing funds but because the conditions are recorded on the Blockchain, they cannot be changed or altered.

Smart contracts allow the implementation of policies for the transfer of all types of assets in a decentralized network. They also add programmability and intelligence to the Blockchain. The smart contract represents a business logic layer, with the actual logic coded in a special high-level language. A smart contract embeds functions that can be invoked by messages that are like function calls. These messages and the input parameters for a single message are specified in a transaction.

For example, consider home mortgage applications. A smart contract could embed all the business logic and intelligence for the rules and regulations needed to allow for automatic computation and initiation of the mortgage application. There may be other conditions besides availability of funds while executing a transaction. For example, our home mortgage smart contract transaction may involve rules, policies, laws, regulations and governing contexts and the verification of employment, funds, etc. The smart contract allows for these other real-world constraints to be realized and implemented on the Blockchain.

This is one of the most interesting and exciting crypto technologies that has huge implications and is set to disrupt many different sectors of our economy that currently use manual contracts.

Chapter 9. Cryptocurrency's Future

Stable coins - A "stable coin" is a cryptocurrency that is pegged to another stable asset such as gold or currency like the dollar. For example, Tether (USDT) is is a "price-stable cryptocurrency" that is "pegged" to the U.S. dollar and is meant to trade for $1 USD. Stable coins are decentralized and not tied to a central bank. These stable coins offer the instant processing and security of payments of cryptocurrencies with the stable valuations of fiat currencies. I believe that we are going to see more stable coins showing up in the crypto space and they are going to be a big addition to how we use cryptocurrencies. You are going to see more and more stable coins appearing as time goes on. Some examples of other stable coins are TrueUSD, USDCoin and the Gemini Dollar. Another new competitor entering this space is JP Morgan's JPM Coin. The JPM Coin is different in that it is a stable coin backed by the dollar. JPM coin will run on a Blockchain network called Quorum, which requires permissions and users that must be approved by JP Morgan. This has many people wondering if the JP Morgan coin is really a cryptocurrency. Facebook recently announced Libra, its stable coin. When released in 2020, Libra is poised to revolutionize how we pay for our goods and services but some people are doubting that the coin will get released. There seems to be a lot of questions about how the coin will be used and the US government is also concerned that the usage of the coin might affect the global economy further weakening fiat currencies. Facebook plans for its users to be able to pay for things or to send money to each other similar to Paypal and Venmo but faster and cheaper. One question many people are asking is will users adopt a centralized stablecoin that keeps track of their financial information? We'll have to see if the government allows this and if the industry accepts and uses Libra when it is released.

Commodity Coins - Bitcoin has legally been defined as a commodity by the CFTC since 2015, referred to as a "virtual commodity" in the category of "exempt commodities" alongside gold, oil and other metal and energy commodities. The commodity-like traits of crypto are one of its greatest value propositions over fiat currencies or even fiat-backed stablecoins and the future will likely see many more cryptocurrencies backed by real commodities like coffee, food, water and common resources like clean air, minerals and energy. Like their real-world counterparts, commodity pegged or backed cryptocurrencies have had lackluster demand so far but this could soon change as commodity prices and demand come off decade long lows and may provide a hedge against USD devaluation and market volatility.

GBC - Government backed Cryptocurrencies - Christine Lagarde, the head of the International Monetary Fund gave a talk at the Singapore Fintech Festival on November 14, 2018. Her talk was titled "Winds of Change: The Case for New Digital Currency". During the talk, she asked a very interesting question. Her question was, "Should central banks issue a new digital form of money"?

She urged the central banks in her speech to be quick with creating their own cryptocurrencies to prevent the system from being taken over by fraudsters and money launderers. She later went on to say that " Various central banks around the world are seriously considering these ideas, including Canada, China, Sweden and Uruguay. They are embracing change and new thinking—as indeed is the IMF."

This was an interesting reversal given that Ms. Lagarde had once slammed Bitcoin and other cryptocurrencies at a previous conference. She now seems to be having a change of view on cryptocurrencies. Christine also stated that "As more and more government institutions investigate the advantages of cryptocurrencies and Blockchain technology, so, too, do they see the potential benefits of having their own state-backed virtual currency. Iran is one such country. They recently announced that they would be introducing their local currency-backed crypto as a means to circumvent U.S. sanctions."

This is very important and cannot be dismissed. By telling central banks to look into creating their own cryptocurrency, she is taking a stand against decentralized cryptos such as Bitcoin.

She tells her audience, "The advantage is clear. Your payment would be immediate, safe, cheap and potentially semi-anonymous… and central banks would retain a sure footing in payment".

Cryptocurrencies Around the World - Cryptocurrencies are used worldwide and governments are having to deal with how to regulate them. Many countries are actively exploring the viability of using cryptocurrencies as a proprietary digital asset within their own financial system. I'm including several countries that are already taking steps in that direction as well as other countries that are approaching cryptocurrencies in other ways that sometimes are in contrast to the way the United States sees cryptocurrencies. One thing is for certain, countries that are not already looking at how they are going to regulate and use cryptocurrencies are going to be left behind.

The United States - The United States is moving cautiously when it comes to cryptocurrencies but is feeling the pressure to accept and adopt a more liberal approach in light of other countries' decisions on how they plan on defining and using them. The US certainly does not want to be left behind and wants to show the world that it is taking a slow but appropriate pace in accepting a world that is rapidly moving more and more into cryptocurrency acceptance. Some states are already beginning to move forward and adopt policies that are cryptocurrency friendly. For example, Businesses can now pay their Ohio taxes with cryptocurrency. Simply sign up your business, enter your tax payment amount and use your Bitcoin wallet to pay the invoice in Bitcoin. Hopefully, more states and the federal government will follow.

Canada - Canada accepts Bitcoin and other cryptocurrencies as a legal way for paying for goods and services and but is viewed as a commodity by the Canada Revenue Agency (CRA). This means that in Canada, cryptocurrency transactions are viewed as barter transactions and the income generated from them is considered as business income. The taxation of Cryptocurrencies also depends whether the individual has is buying and selling cryptocurrencies or is buying them as investments.

Belgium - Belgium is one of many countries that has no restrictions on the use of Bitcoin or other cryptocurrencies. The Belgian government does not consider cryptocurrencies to be a threat to the economic stability of the country. The Financial Services and Markets Authority (FSMA) has given Bitcoin a value-added tax exempt status by classifying it as a financial service. It is no required to have a license to issue cryptocurrencies and they are not subject to any regulatory supervision but you do have to pay taxes on any cryptocurrency income. Currently that tax is 33% of your income.

Dubai - Dubai is one of several countries whose government is launching a government-backed cryptocurrency. In 2018, Dubai officially launched EmCash.The launch gave retailers

Point of Sale devices that will accept the new EmCash cryptocurrency. Consumers can now pay their bills, retail purchases, mobile phone bills, school fees and other utilities using the government-backed cryptocurrency according to local media outlet TradeArabia[38]. EmCash is issued by the Credit Bureau of Dubai which is a subsidiary of the Dubai Department of Economic Development and is a new use of government backed cryptocurrencies. These "municipal" cryptocurrencies are launched by cities to be used for all sorts of city related projects such as their plan to create the world's first passport-free airport. They also offer their citizens a lower entry to invest in certain projects, goods and services while also helping their governments in the funding of projects. Think of them as "crypto bonds". Other cities are already exploring this alternative funding method as well.

Venezuela - Venezuela launched its state-owned cryptocurrency, the Petro, in October of 2018. The Petro can be purchased directly from the country's treasury via the coin's official website http://petro.gob.ve or from six crypto exchanges authorized by the government. The coin can be purchased for Yuan, Euro and U.S. dollars, or for certain cryptocurrencies, by legal entities and individuals who have registered and passed a validation process on the coin's official website. The government has also started offering a cryptocurrency remittance service available on the government's Patria remittance website.

---

[38] http://www.tradearabia.com/news/BANK_346022.html

The Superintendency of Cryptoassets and Related Activities (Sunacrip), the main regulator of all crypto activities in Venezuela, announced the launch of the service on its Patria portal[39] in March 2019. According to its website, to use the service and receive crypto remittances, "the natural person must be registered with the Patria platform, be of legal age and reside in the Bolivarian Republic of Venezuela." Senders, however, can be outside of Venezuela.

In addition, the only cryptocurrencies that can be used to send [remittances] are Bitcoin and litecoin. On July 4, 2019, Venezuela's President Nicolas Maduro ordered the country's leading bank, Banco de Venezuela, to begin to accept the Petro, the nation's cryptocurrency, at all of its branches. Venezuela is an example of a country that is trying to have an economy that can use two legal currencies concurrently hoping to be able to transition from its failing fiat to its new cryptocurrency.

Zimbabwe - While many governments are still trying to figure out whether cryptocurrencies are a good thing, the authorities of Zimbabwe have decided that in their case, they are. Zimbabwe suffers from racial and ethnic conflicts, dictatorship and poor education. The Zimbabwean economy provides a very low gross domestic product per capita and Zimbabwe continues to struggle with the high inflation that continues to hurt its economy, to the point where it's switched to US

---

[39] https://.patria.org.ve

dollars. In 2009, Inflation in Zimbabwe reached 80 billion percent making their currency virtually worthless. Now, currencies like Bitcoin and Litecoin are being considered as potential options to help restore some confidence in the Zimbabwean economy. Zimbabwe is poorly developed in technology but their mobile phone penetration is at 93% as of early 2019. This along with the fact that the government has issued no laws about cryptocurrency means that Bitcoin and other cryptocurrencies are legal to use in Zimbabwe at least unofficially.

Switzerland - A recent report in Avenir Suisse[40] sees an opportunity for the Swiss financial industry. The reports suggests that Switzerland consider developing a country stablecoin. Having such a coin could position Switzerland internationally as a pioneer in trading tokenized securities and become a major player in the trading of crypto assets.

Digitec-Galaxus[41], the 'Amazon' of Switzerland, now accepts Bitcoin and other select cryptocurrencies as a means of payment. Switzerland has been a hotbed for Bitcoin adoption and the Blockchain industry. It regularly hosts cryptocurrency events and its stock exchange has rolled out cryptocurrency-tied products such as a Bitcoin ETP.

---

[40] developing a stablecoin could convert Switzerland into a "Blockchain nation
[41] https://www.galaxus.ch/en

The country is also home to many crypto startups who have found a home in the Swiss city of Zug, also known as 'Crypto valley.' What's more, residents of the city can even pay for municipal services in Bitcoin. Even train tickets for the country's Federal railway system can be bought for Bitcoin at every station kiosk.In November of 2018, Switzerland's leading stock exchange gave the go-ahead for the world's first cryptocurrency ETP.

The Marshall Islands - The Marshall Islands is an island country located in the Pacific Ocean and consists of five individual islands and 29 atolls. For the previous 40 years, the country had been administered by the United States, as part of the Trust Territory of the Pacific islands, but the Islands attained independence in 1986 under the Compact of Free Association[42].

Currently, the Marshall Islands uses the U.S. dollar as its official currency but is actively working on creating its own digital currency called the Sovereign (SOV). Once issued, the SOV will circulate alongside the US dollar, thus making the Marshall Islands a country with two coexisting legal tenders Either currency can be used by its users for purchases goods and services, paying debts and taxes.

---

[42] https://en.wikipedia.org/wiki/Compact_of_Free_Association

Chapter 10. Interesting Cryptocurrencies Worth Watching

I've included a list of some cryptocurrencies that have some interesting use cases, a viable product, a strong management team and a fairly large market cap. You might want to take a look at them. I have included a short description of each one. It will be interesting to see where they are a year from now. Full Disclosure: I am not offering investment advice here. These are simply some of the cryptocurrencies that I personally like and may hold from time to time.

Bitcoin (BTC) - Bitcoin is the world's first digital currency. Bitcoin can be used to send money directly to anyone, anywhere in the world. Many people feel that because Bitcoin was the first cryptocurrency and has the largest market cap, it is going to continue to be the dominant and most popular Bitcoin and will continue to increase in value. As of September 2019 , BTC was ranked 1st on the list of largest cryptocurrencies by market capitalization.

Dash (DASH) - Dash is a peer-to-peer decentralized electronic cash system that was built upon Bitcoin's core code with the addition of some additional features that were lacking in Bitcoin, such as privacy and fast transaction times. It is one of the most promising alternative coins to Bitcoin and is very popular with retailers wanting to accept a cryptocurrency in their business. The creators of Dash combined the words digital and cash to come up with the name. Transactions using the Dash network are instantaneous, private and very secure.

In January 2019, Dash upgraded its network to version 0.13. It can now confirm transactions in roughly 1.3 seconds. That's huge for merchants, because payments in DASH are now virtually immediate. Just like Bitcoin, Dash has its own Blockchain, its own wallets and is open-source. It also has a very large and active community of users and developers.

To quote their website[43], *"In Dash, everyone has a voice and the ability to propose projects directly to the network. Anything you can do - from marketing to development - that helps Dash grow and improve can be funded. This means Dash funds its own growth and adoption, consensus is guaranteed and everyone is accountable to the network."*

Several countries are looking at Dash as an alternative way of allowing the payments of goods and services. As of February 2019, Venezuela led the way with over 2500 merchants that accept Dash as payment for goods such as food, electronics, apparel, health, beauty, medicine, sports and travel. As of September 2019, DASH was ranked 17th on the list of largest cryptocurrencies by market capitalization.

---

[43]https://www.dash.org/

Ether (ETH) - Ether is the native cryptocurrency of the Ethereum Blockchain and is an open source, public, Blockchain-based distributed computing platform and operating system featuring smart contract scripting functionality. Ethereum was proposed in late 2013 by Vitalik Buterin, a cryptocurrency researcher and programmer. He funded the development of Ethereum by an online crowd sale that took place between July and August of 2014. Ethereum then went live on 30 July 2015, with 72 million coins "premined". This accounts for about 68% of the total circulating supply in 2019.

In 2016, as a result of the exploitation of a flaw in The DAO project's smart contract software and subsequent theft of $50 million worth of Ether, Ethereum was split into two separate Blockchains. The new separate version became Ethereum (ETH) with the theft reversed and the original continued as Ethereum Classic (ETC)[44]. As of September 2019, ETH was ranked 2nd on the list of largest cryptocurrencies by market capitalization.

EOS - is a popular Blockchain that uses the EOSIO protocol. It is also the name of the Blockchain's system token. EOS is one of many Ethereum alternatives but also one of the most promising. Block One, a company located in the Cayman Islands, launched the project in 2017, as a new Blockchain project that also has the ability to handle smart contracts. But

---

[44] https://en.wikipedia.org/wiki/Ethereum

more than just smart contracts, EOS's vision is to offer the most powerful infrastructure for decentralized applications (Dapps). The goal of EOS is to be the fastest, cheapest and most scalable smart contract Blockchain in the crypto space. According to the EOS white paper, there will be NO transaction fees to pay when sending and receiving funds using EOS. The reason they are able to do this is that unlike Ethereum and its Proof of Work model, EOS does things differently.

As people help verify transactions, they are rewarded out of newly created EOS coins. EOS uses a consensus mechanism used to support the network called Delegated Proof of Stake (or DPoS). As of September 2019, EOS was ranked 8th on the list of largest cryptocurrencies by market capitalization.

Stellar (XLM) - According to the stellar website, "Stellar is a platform that connects banks, payment systems and people and integrates to move money quickly, reliably and at almost no cost". Their main competitor is Ripple (XRP) but the main difference between the two cryptos is the fact that Stellar is decentralized while Ripple is not. Stellar has joined forces with IBM and recently announced and launched Blockchain World Wire. Running on the Stellar network, the service will be used to settle cross-border payments in real-time. There are also a number of stablecoins already being used on the network. Wirex, for example, is a cryptocurrency and debit card app that plans to be the next-generation multi-currency travel card.

When it is released, the Wirex Visa card will automatically convert more than 18 digital currencies and traditional currencies at the point of sale, letting you seamlessly spend your crypto and multiple currencies in real life, anywhere Visa is accepted.[45] As of September 2019, XLM was ranked 11th on the list of largest cryptocurrencies by market capitalization.

Steem - Steem has often been described as a smart media token. The cryptocurrency allows people to produce and share digital content. Community members can then vote and reward those content producers with Steem tokens. Steemit Inc., a privately held company based in New York City was started on March 24, 2016 by Ned Scott and Dan Larimer. Steem has over 1.2 million registered accounts and a daily volume of more than a million signed operations. It's blockchain has one of the highest levels of online activity. In terms of total market capitalization, STEEM is currently ranked 75th with a market capitalization of more than 111 million. (September 2019).

Monero (XMR) - Monero is a cryptocurrency that's focused on privacy, fungibility and decentralization. The token was created in 2014 and was one of a few alt coins that was able to survive the 2014-2015 crypto bear market mainly due to its privacy design. The Monero protocol provides users with privacy through the implementation of three core cryptographic techniques: stealth addresses, ring signatures and ring confidential transactions. These techniques obscure not only

---

[45] https://wirexapp.com/global

the transaction's sender and recipient, but also the amount of the transaction. As of September 2019, XMR was ranked 10th on the list of largest cryptocurrencies by market capitalization.

Zcash (ZEC) - Zcash is a Blockchain and cryptocurrency which allows private transactions in a public Blockchain. It was developed in response to some of Bitcoin's shortcoming. It uses the same algorithm as Bitcoin but improved on it by enabling semi-transparent processing. Zcash also uses a mathematical technique called a zero-knowledge proof to conduct its Blockchain transactions. The proofs ensure that the transaction's contents remaine anonymous even though the transaction is publicly visible on a decentralized ledger. This gives the user of Zcash the best of both worlds. Users get enhanced privacy but can also verify transactions without knowing the identity of the transaction makers or the amount being transferred. Coinbase has recently announced that its customers can now buy, sell, send, receive and store Zcash. As of September 2019, ZEC was ranked 28th on the list of largest cryptocurrencies by market capitalization.

IOTA (MIOTA) - is a crypto token specially designed and optimized for the Internet-of-Things (IoT) The main innovation behind the IOTA system is Tangle, their directed acyclic graph (DAG) based ledger. In DAG-based cryptocurrencies there are no blocks. "Consensus and validation are decided by the whole network of active participants. This makes it so that everyone has an equal say in the network regarding the transaction making process. Since it doesn't use blocks, the ledger can transfer value without any fees. Consensus is no longer decoupled, but instead, it's an intrinsic part of the system (unlike modern Blockchains). This leads to a decentralized and self-regulated peer-to-peer network."[46] MIOTA is a unit of IOTA. It is bought directly on almost all exchanges and the price of IOTA is usually quoted in MIOTA. The "M" stands for mega, so 1 MIOTA is equivalent to 1,000,000 IOTA. As of September 2019, MIOTA was ranked 19th on the list of largest cryptocurrencies by market capitalization.

Brave (BAT) - The Basic Attention Token is an open-source, decentralized ad exchange platform that uses the Ethereum blockchain. The platform is integrated with a web browser called Brave. The browser gives users a safer, faster and better browsing experience but Brave is much more than a browser. Brave supports content creators by paying them with Brave Payment tokens. The Brave browser allows users to tip websites and content creators with BAT tokens thereby supporting the content creators on the sites they visit. The Brave browser does not track or store browsing data and loads pages twice as fast as Chrome and Firefox. I highly suggest you try it out. As of September 2019, BAT was ranked 34nd on the list of largest cryptocurrencies by market capitalization.

Tron TRX - Tron is a third-generation Blockchain-based decentralized platform that plans to build a free, global digital content entertainment system with distributed storage

---

[46] https://cryptalker.com/iota-miota/

technology, that will also allow an easy and cost-effective way of sharing of digital content. The Tron network uses its own cryptocurrency called Tronix (TRX). Tronix is the basic unit of account in Tron's Blockchain and It is the currency that pays you for your content. Using Tron cryptocurrency's ecosystem, you can share content with other people, but you are also compensated as a content creator for the content and data that you create. This model is the opposite of how traditional social media companies like Facebook monetize user data. Tron crypto empowers artists and content creators all over the world into having ownership over the content they produce. As of September 2019, TRX was ranked 15th on the list of largest cryptocurrencies by market capitalization.

Factom FCT - Factom, Inc., established in 2014, was started in part to solve the problem of how to validate software that was going into products, systems and servers as well as trying to solve the issue of how to prove digital identities. The Factom team realized at the time that there was not a global trustable registry and saw the need. To quote Paul Snow, CEO of Factom, "We started Factom to build a more honest and transparent world. We create software that makes it impossible to change the past and solves valuable honesty, trust and audit-related business problems."[47] Factum is designed to separate the enabling technology that Bitcoin has, the immutable ledger from the coin application.

---

[47] https://www.factom.com/company/about-us/

They accomplished this by creating a two token system. First they created a Bitcoin type of token technology and second, they created a hyperledger like technology. The Hyperledger technology burns tradable tokens and the user receives a non-tradable token called an entry credit. The Bitcoin type-token pays incentives to everyone using the network. These tokens can be also be exchanged for fiat or other cryptocurrencies on many exchanges. Factom's factoid is the tradable token that gives people incentives to work in the factom infrastructure ecosystem. Factom is currently working with the Department of Homeland Security and with the Bill and Melinda Gates Foundation. As of September 2019, FCT was ranked 104th on the list of largest cryptocurrencies by market capitalization.

Final Thoughts - The Future of Cryptocurrencies

I would like to leave you all with some final thoughts about what I see happening in the near future. First, I hope that this book has helped you understand cryptocurrencies and why it is important that you not only understand them but get actively involved with them. Just like the Internet revolution, The cryptocurrency revolution is here and you need to be a part of it.

Think about this for a second. Are you compensated right now from advertisers who know what you read, what you watch while streaming a video on the Internet, what you watch on TV, where you shop, destinations you visit, places you eat? Do you realize how much information Apple, Microsoft, Google and Facebook have on you? All of the information that is collected by these companies is of extreme interest to advertisers and marketers. What if you could decide what marketers and advertisers have access your shopping, reading and buying habits and they paid you for those rights? What if you could share your medical information with only the medical personnel that needed them.

The fact we are not currently compensated for any of this information should bother everyone. Cryptocurrencies have the ability to turn the tables on these companies. There are already alternatives to social media sites like FaceBook, browsers like

Google Chrome, informational sites like Wikipedia, video sharing sites like YouTube, travel sites like ARBO, ride-sharing sites like Uber, all offering and using Blockchain and cryptocurrency technologies.

Remember that Bitcoin is only 10 years old. It is still at the early age of being adopted. The average person is just now starting to hear about Bitcoins and cryptocurrencies. Fewer have yet to recognize the importance of the Blockchain, smart contracts, Bitcoin, cryptocurrencies and other related technologies such as the Internet of Things (IoT) and Artificial Intelligence (AI). All of these technologies are going to affect all parts of your everyday life and many already are so knowing and understanding them is something that you should start doing right now.

Steve Lee, the Former Product Director of Google stated that due to the fixed supply of Bitcoin (21 million), "If you own 0.28 BTC and HODL, you can be certain no more than 1% of the current world's population can ever own more BTC than you".

Due to the fixed supply of Bitcoin, only 1% of the world's population can own more than 0.28 BTC. As of July 2019, you can purchase that .28 Bitcoin for $2900 and become part of the 1% of the current world population that will ever be able to own Bitcoin.

If you only take away one nugget of information from this book it is the fact in the first 10 years of Bitcoin's existence, it has grown from $0 to over $11,000. In 2010, you could have bought 10 Bitcoins for $100. Those Bitcoins would now be worth $117,660.00 as of August 2019.

One satoshi is the smallest unit of a Bitcoin and is one hundred millionths of a single Bitcoin or .00000001. Currently, one satoshi is worth 0.00011766 US Dollars. This does not seem like a lot until you put the amount in perspective. The Iranian Rial is worth 0.000030 US Dollars, the Indonesian Rupiah is 0.000070 US Dollars and the Usbekistan Som is worth 0.00011 US Dollars and finally, the Vietnamese Dong is worth 0.000043 US Dollars.

It's amazing that a digital currency that is not backed by any country is worth more than some country's own fiat currency! Think about that.

One final observation. Take a look at the chart below from Coin Market Cap. It shows the value of Bitcoin from 2013 to August of 2019.

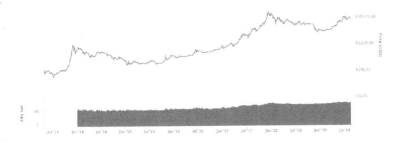

Notice the trend. Bitcoin has gone up from $135 to over $10,000 in the past 6 years. This is an incredible statistic that many people are not aware of.

What would happen if you decided to buy $100 worth of Bitcoin today? Well there are several scenarios. Either the price of Bitcoin is going to drop to nothing and you lose your $100, or it stays at $100 and you break even or it continues to go up. I am inclined to believe that it will continue to go up due to increased usage, acceptance and adoption. Yes there will be corrections and dips like many assets but it is an impressive fact that over the past 6 years, Bitcoin has out preformed other assets such as gold and silver as well as many stocks and mutual funds.

Should you purchase some Bitcoin? I obviously can't tell you but I hope that this book has made you more aware of Bitcoin, crptocurrencies, the Blockchain and how they will affect us all in the future. Maybe its a good idea to start looking into a crypto IRA and putting some cryptocurrencies like Bitcoin and Ethereum periodically in them as a retirement vehicle. Just a thought.

Finally, with cryptocurrencies, the Blockchain and smart contracts, we will soon have the option to become our own individual, private database of information and we will be able to decide who gets access to it. We will be able to monetize ourselves and we will be able to determine how our information is used and if we want to share and at what price. We will finally be able to take back our privacy.

It may be too late for the current generation because we have already surrendered most of our data to Google, Facebook, Apple and Microsoft but it may not be too late for the next generation to take back their data and finally decide how it will be used.

ABOUT THE AUTHOR

Fito Kahn is the owner of Multimedia Partners, LLC, an Austin, Texas based Web development agency. He is a Senior Drupal Developer and Trainer, Project Manager and IT Support Specialist and has been involved in the computer industry for over 30 years. He received his Bachelor of Science degree in Communications from the University of Texas in Austin and a Masters degree in Media Studies from the New School University in New York. Fito is also a cryptocurrency enthusiast and evangelist and has been involved in the cryptocurrency industry since 2015. He regularly attends cryptocurrency conferences and shares his thoughts on the cryptocurrency industry, as well as relevant crypto news on his website, cryptocurrencyinfo.today.

When Fito is not working on cryptocurrency projects or building websites, you can find him playing the guitar or his congas and spending time with his family.

Please Stay in Contact

Because cryptocurrencies are relatively new and the space is evolving, it is important that you stay up to date with what is happening. If you enjoyed my book, go to my website. I have instructions on where and how to buy Bitcoin, how to setup your wallet and what you can do with cryptos today. You should also sign up to receive my newsletter. By signing up you will have access to periodic, exclusive and timly reports on other crypto topics and also get advanced notice and special pricing on other books as they come out. Future books will cover topics such as Cryptocurrency Investing Strategies, Staking Cryptocurrencies, Dapps and Cryptocurrencies, Crypto Mining, The Future of Artificial Intelligence, Cryptos and IoT's(The Internet of Things), Dataism and Dataistic networks.

Subscribe to my newsletter - Go to
www.cryptocurrencyinfo.today

Follow me on FaceBook - Go to
https://www.facebook.com/fito.kahn

Connect with me on LinkedIn - Go to
https://www.linkedin.com/in/fitokahn/